Connexions

Poems by Marie Gilbert
Drawings by Mimi Baruch

St. Andrews College Press
Laurinburg, NC

ACKNOWLEDGMENTS

Some of these poems have appeared in *The Pilot, A Carolina Literary Companion, International Poetry Review, Library Journal, St. Andrews/Sandhills Review, Pembroke Magazine, Crucible, Mt. Olive Review, Fire, Crescent Observer, Cairn, Poetry Society of South Carolina, The Edge of Our World, Coastal Cruising, Signs along the Way, Green River Review, The Wayah Review, Manna, Bay Leaves, Weymouth Anthology, and The Arts Journal.*

© Copyright 1994 by Marie Gilbert

Cover Art and Illustrations by Mimi Baruch

Published by: St. Andrews College Press
                     1700 Dogwood Mile
                     Laurinburg, NC 28352

Printed by: Atlantic Printing
                     Tabor City N. C.

ISBN: 1-879934-28-0

First Printing: December 1994

PART ONE

....near landfall
now and then

FOG

Morning head on the pillow
I lie in the house by the Saint Lucie River.
Boat traffic tunnels through mountains of fog,
horns seem to come from anywhere
in the zero visibility.

Fog horns moan, Captains listen
for one blast or two,
pass port to port as hands
feel ahead in blind-man's bluff
though fog is no game for guessers.

Let the river be life.
We cruise, say "Good morning,"
listen to the word, read the inflection
guess the signal to come on, move over, move on.
I am well, I am ill, friendly or withdrawn.

We guess and feel our way
hope inflection matches words –
mine as well as yours.

Ever since the first grunt from caveman lips
pierced the fog of primal dawn
man has grappled with the puzzle of man.

Marie Gilbert

CLUSTERING:
GALACTIC AND PERSONAL

Fifteen billion years ago, the universe was young
stars and galaxies spread evenly.

Now we're told galaxies clump cluster
in space to leave voids between.

We struggle to conquer voids, fight
natural gravities with trifling strength

reach out of our phylum
into titanic holes that swallow voice.

Super voids grow vast
galactic clusters, dense.

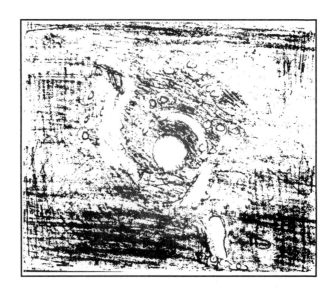

FAMILY PORTRAIT

You watch from above the mantel
in an easiness I never saw
through the veil of flesh and bone.
A silk peony gentles your chin
chiffon floats from quiet shoulders.

As a bride I felt your chiseled kiss,
stiff heavy silk
and high lace collars.
I swished my blond bob
hoping to mask my terror.

You brought up fine sons
I am the wife of one, and
your husband proclaimed your quality
until the day he died.

You and I called across an ocean,
carefully navigated
tides, currents, waves,
came near landfall
now and then
in an endless voyage.

Marie Gilbert

LISTENING AT THE IXORA HEDGE

Snipping here, down deep there
she lowers the hedge gently
deftly saving the natural shape.
Echoes float up from silence.
She hears the crusty gardener specify
"I box it off low!", hears her father
answer, "My daughter likes the blossoms."
She pauses in her trimming to smile, knowing
next she'll hear, "No need to have the flowers."

This man would shoot a mockingbird
for singing when men should sleep, a cardinal
for pecking fruit. A falling leaf was dirty.
Fractious, he slither-eyed the neighbors
who paused at the gate
to watch the sun slip into the pool.

The father tried a time or two but wasn't one
to waste his words, especially when he was old
he worked with what he had, a man
who held many jobs he left or lost.

At funeral time the gardener comes
scowling at scion who wish
not to weep in public.
He stays through the very private time,
the reading of the will, and then
proclaims, veiled in eulogy,
not one of them will ever measure up.

They would have worked with him, somehow.
Now, they watch him walk away.

MEETING YOU IS NO BAD THING

Lives brush against lives
down the line in the folk dance:

I clasp the hand of a man overflowing
in grief convincing real for wife so rude
while she lived no one came to call
that was invited in, or ever came again.
Perhaps he alone had entry
to the center of a chambered nautilus,
knew it rich and rare, well worth the trip
round and round her rind. Or, perhaps
she was the shell of his defense. Now, she's gone,
like a naked snail he melts in the light of day.

I meet a girl talking and talking
as if she finds listeners too dull to speak,
must save them from embarrassment,
or, talking tamps her secret sin
that might surface, should silence settle.

Another girl, with warts beneath her nose,
uneasily watches her husband charm
his way around the room.

Hand to hand we're passed along.
Layer after layer sorts itself.

Marie Gilbert

HUMANITIES ONE:
FOR A CHILD ON VACATION
AT BLACK MOUNTAIN NORTH CAROLINA

The Depression hangs thick as coal dust
clings like thin clothes in icy weather.
Loaded coal cars wait to be tunneled
shoved and tugged over and down the mountain
to Marion and Old Fort.

The child waits on the curb of a paved street
in front of gift shops and the A&P
peers with her low-to-the-ground sight
beneath four tracks of coal haulers
to the dirt street on the other side.
She sees a girl about her size but slimmer
slip barefoot from a house
that might not last the winter,
duck under, even touch the giant wheels,
climb the ladder between the cars
glance right and left, then reach so high
her thin shift slides above her knees
to fill with coal the sack she hugs,
struggle down, duck quickly, scurry home.

The child watching from the curb pictures
a Franklin stove, embers dying near supper time.

Her Mother steps out of the A&P.
Hand in hand through the woods lane
they walk past McGraw Coffee House
to the trim cottage, theirs for the summer.
"Mother, she stole that coal?" She wonders,
feels her Mother's interest
tells all she saw or imagined

listens carefully to her own telling
begins to ponder human matters.

REVERSING THE SENSES

Only with a touch will I speak,
my eyes are closed to see
the oriole pour
glass marbles from his throat,
the martin cling to his porch,
or, if that is wing breath,
hover above his roof.

Oak limbs
weave vermilion on eyelids,
drop messages
that brown unread.

11

Marie Gilbert

DEAR COUSIN

The closeness that you seek would have been
easy when we lived in your town where
swinging on the porch of our rented house
was the big pleasure of our life.

Even though we worked long hours
there was evening time
and months quite often
longer than our funds.

We understand you couldn't ask us
to so small a wedding. We would like
to meet your wife and think it nice
our daughters share an age.

Yes, we'd love to have you visit.
Our country house has trails, barns, horses.
You would like it best, I think
when we refill the pool

next summer, I will try
to save some visiting time.
Demands are heavy, weekends precious
but I agree that families should stay close.

MI KWAY NIM ROANOAK

(Mi kway nim means 'remember' in the modern dialect of Ojibway
of the Algonquin language spoken on the Carolina coast.)

English skin white as the Cliffs of Dover
tends the iron pot on the tripod over embers
coral by dark, gray by light of day.

Smoke drifts, smoke seeps
through wattle and wood to rest under roof thatch
 permeate the packed clay floor

dim the sleek yellow satin of hair
pulled back into a knot
tight as necessity.

A wooden pail bounces on rope in her fingers
on the way to the spring for drinking water
cuts on return, heavy as hogshead.

She rinses her face with drinking water
quickly, when no one sees,
one frivolity in a hard new land.

Small and neat she stretches up
to seem tall as cliffs - knowing
through the smoke, he sees

mi kway nim
at Roanoak.

Marie Gilbert

TWENTY YEARS BEYOND ROANOAK

"At Ritanoe *** Gepanacon preserved seven of the English alive,
four men, two boys and one young maid, and fled up the river of
Choanoke to beat his copper." The words of an Indian quoted from
published work of Wm. Starchy, London, 1610

You are the youngest of our men, and I
am old for this land at sixty-one.
Just fifteen you sailed from England,
worked stouthearted as any man.

Mi kway nim, remember, mi kway nim
from Roanoak, the ship sailed back for supplies
taking our core. Like confused birds migrating
we flew north in autumn, to the Chesepiuc -

a gentle people still outside the nation
ruled by Powhatan. They took us in.
We shared our skill with copper, learned of corn,
lived as one, our people and the Indian.

When Powhatan heard the new prophecy
that his kingdom would fall to invaders
the flashing sails of Spanish probes
fueled his fear, mi kway nim.

Perhaps sighting English searching for us
triggered the massacre
the leveling of Chesepiuc. I wonder
you and I will ever know.

We seven escaped to the Chowanoaks
refuged at Ritanoe with Gepanacon.
Up the river we beat his copper,
we live, mi kway nim,

we ply our skill under Virginia sun
on this ridge in April blue
we turn to copper, darken
with sweat over annealing fires.

The maiden with us sees
the young brave often pass,
her eyes follow, her white face smiles
she bronzes from within.

The boys learn to use the bow
take to chipping stone with flint
soon they'll hunt for larger game
be counted with the braves.

Slaves of Gepanacon, you complain?
Orders you have taken well
but you shipped out to sea too early
to have felt the cutting edge of freedom.

In this wilderness would we flee
a day's run deep through lands of Powhatan
seeking rumored settlement, chancing
if find it at all, to find it Spanish?

Once we carved crosses and signs on trees
whispered of ducks floating on the Thames
of mist rolling into South Hampton
mi kway nim

now we understand Ojibway
hear talk of hunting
put our trust in the corn crop
share the fear of Powhatan.

Marie Gilbert

Should John White himself find us
bronzed and wearing skins
would he know his colonists?
Would we see him kinsman?

I dream, oh yes, I dream of full sails
wind fresh on each ear, and "Land ho."
I hear carriage wheels on cobblestones
awake, startled, by the rumble.

Mi kway nim, mi kway nim

SACKCLOTH

Your apology
though I never took it as such
came stylishly dressed
in high design affection.

Warmth exuded from you to me
and me to you.
The deepening of friendship
I took it for

until I learned
what you had done.

Marie Gilbert

IN THE BASEMENT OF
A BURNING HOUSE

I dream the basement with stone stairs
narrow as a tunnel
we must climb –
the smoke and fire.
Others in the family move in slow motion
faceless.

Rosa comes down the stairs to help,
spilling over the third step
where she sits
and is stuck –
her neat blue uniform, white cap
and apron where clean black hands rest –
wedged in the exit.

I push and pry, "Turn around"
I cry and wonder if she tries!
I struggle with her ponderous form
smell the starch that crisps her apron
even while the smoke grows thicker
the flames closer.

"I'll have to climb over you."
As her smooth face puzzles, I add
"And pull you from the other side
or we will both be lost."

I begin to climb over bare arms
and soft human parts
clothed in blue and white.

The scene blurs.
"Let me go back", I plead
"To be sure I pulled her free."

SUMMONS TO A RETIREMENT HOME IN FLORIDA

I mumble that he would want it
this or that way –
a way to control my grief,

plan the service for myself
call it my last act for him
though he'd want simple and the easiest.

I soak up the sunshine
that lengthened his time,
bathe in the warmth of his friends
the remnant of his aura.

These letters left for me?
I'll read them as if he were here,

after that, I'll get on
with the arrangements.

Marie Gilbert

STRANGE ENSLAVEMENT

(on reading <u>Widow's Trial</u> - John Ehle)

The bride knows his kiss
his knuckles and steel ring
the brass of his belt buckle.

She gnaws and fidgets at lips lapping
over gums with new empty spaces
and broken teeth,

speaks
as learning a language
"I do, yes, I do"

Wedding guests weep silently
having said all they can.
Helpless, they hope for the best.

She carries her homemade trousseau
in a cardboard case
and, follows him.

THE UNTHINKING BOOR

Your words leave me wet behind the visible eye
bone and marrow raw to the elements.
With quick breaths to shore up
I shamble
sans clothes, skin or flesh –
bones only –
marrow leaking from joints.
Clenched lips bleed for your departure.

Marie Gilbert

CONVERSATION WITH A BROOK
(THE CAUTION AND THE COMPLAINT)

This rock is Spartan bed
odd to find comfort here
for listening.
White swirls ask,
"Where do you go?"
In answer, my prospects skip
rainbows on the water.
The brook slows
to murmur cautions, cautions
only to spine my shining troop.
Over a granite lip
thin water sheets, sighs.
"Infant stream with old man wisdom!"
I claim out of settling chill,
"I'll inch my line across the map."

Rounding a worn rock
gray gurgling whimpers,
"What of me?"
I grab up my rainbows,
rise to proclaim,
"I struggle with choices, but you –
your course is set."
To Troublesome Creek where
Washington's horse was shod
at the foundry there, you'll sing
past farmer's fields, pastures
where cows wade to drink,
into the Haw. In the sun
you'll swell to woods and fields,
rest dotted with ducks and sailing boats.

Mills you'll turn
all in stride, pour your sum
into the Cape Fear, mighty water
of Wilmington shipping,
shrimp boats, fisher folk.
The depth, the width
the length of run is known from the start."

The brook trickles over a pebbled bed,
a lamentation rises
into the misty air.

Marie Gilbert

WHO ARE YOU

Ou ah ou, the dove coos in early morning.
Missy begins to live out the answer even before
she knows of the question. Her skirt flips
as she scurries from cheerleading to drama club
after classes in French, English, History and math.
Arms cradle books. As a dry sponge on a wet day
she gathers resources unto herself.

Ou ah ou filters through window lace.
"I am bride," the eager answer comes.
Today I give myself to him, we will be one.
Even his faults, those precious few,
will be one with my faults.

Ou ah ou comes with the rising sun.
A small head nestles under the curve of her chin.
"I am Mother," she whispers to herself
and to the babe born already knowing.
Protective as a dog with willing teeth
she pads on soft feet.

Ou ah ou comes with hot gray light
moist when fever melts resolve. "I am weak,
wounded," she breathes from her bed.
Oh, doves, she is with broken wing.
Call softly while she heals.

Ou ah Ou, she strokes the drapery to shield
the weary eyes of her dreaming mate.
"I am tiger." She who had suckled the cubs
set them out to play, purrs
as she darkens the den.

Ou ah ou ou ou.

CHUCK-WILL'S-WIDOW

Unfortunate bird
saddled with the species
nightjar, goatsucker,
still fills the air
with sapphires on black satin.

Chuck-will's widow –
here, over there
will's widow
chuck-will's-widow.

I find one nesting
in twigs on the ground,
awkward, unredeemable,

so she proclaims to the dark
in the voice of chuck and will's widow
all the deep shadow wisdom
somehow spoken in the loud and in the soft
of the same words over and over poured
into the waning night.

PLIGHT OF THE GOOSE

Centered in the blush of the lake at dawn
the curves of his neck waltz
with his mirrored image.

No cute goose this,
no red ribbon and holly sprig;
nor does he stir thoughts of the platter.

Like stagehands in the wings, branches
peek through mist folding water's edge
backdrop for center stage.
Morning's silver shafts floodlight the ballet.

The goose moves inspired, aware of his moment.
His agreeable partner follows perfectly
as he sways to wind whispers.

He finds himself alone with his shadow
center stage. The show is on
with no rehearsal time.

Alas poor goose:
stagehands peer
spotlights smile and glisten
music whispers
his dance flows on
invincible, he thinks,
I should sing.

His only voice somewhere
between a bark and a quack,
raucous for bawdy backroom stories.

Mists lift revealing weeds and trunks of trees
wind pushes waves to erode the clay-red shore
the mirror cracks to ripples.

Marie Gilbert

SPEECH LESSON FROM
THE VEGETABLE MAN

Hair more blue than black
smooth as his mocha skin,
he approaches as if walking
were a gift to Seminoles.
I select tomatoes and ask
"Where did you grow these?"

Small silence before he sings it
"ImMOKalee"
whispery as its place on the map
empty spot south
of the Caloosahatchee
between Okeechobee and Punta Rassa.

ImMOKalee
I had seen the name
pronounced it IMmoKAlee.

From generations tuned
to rain and sun,
to vibrations in the soil
springs the sound ImMOKalee.

Over and over I tongue
the amber honey
taste the breeze shape
try to speak the undulation.

Marie Gilbert

POSSESSION: THE FICUS TREE

Up through stories of limbs, I see
just enough blue to know sky exists
above this spot kept dry by masses of tiny green.

Brown cast-offs drop a crisp carpet
over roots heaving "like pythons" –
cables to sanctum deep within earth.

A troop of apes would find ample space
up in these elephant trunks wrinkled at joints,
curved ready to breathe.

Three decades ago hurricane winds toppled
it into the river. To right the tree
we hired a dragline, built a sea wall.

Here where the Saint Lucie leads
to Lake Okeechobee, the Caloosahatchee
and on to Fort Myers

yachtsmen point their tack
by the high and dark green easy to see,
bargemen peer ahead as if watching for a friend.

A lonely heron sleeps up there.
If we walk beneath at night, he squawks.
We try to remember.

TEN P.M. IN BUCHAREST

Light from the Intercontinental
shafts into the wet dark.
We fumble down the few steps to the street
toward the yellow glow of the bus

eyes adjust slowly
a few boys push postcards.

One with pale hair comes near
his hands cupped waist high.

Slim face up to me he says one word, "Lady?"
Habit does not fit:
I should take him, too small
to be out of bed at this hour,
to the light of the bus
have band-aids handy
a cup of milk
let him talk.

I hear the driver's
harsh tones say "Be gone."

The tour guide cautions, "Careful,
I can tag luggage but not children."

World of many fences,
someone small wanders
the dark streets of Bucharest.

31

PART TWO

....a close world barely turning.

GOLDEN PROSPECTS

My hand cradled
in the small of your back
rises and falls with your sleeping-breath.

Nothing exists
beyond the night
cocooning a close world
barely turning.

Dogs hunt in rhythmical barking
that drifts from hills
blends with autumn crickets.

Wrapped in warmth
I wait for
the widening of day.

Marie Gilbert

A LOVE OF CONTRASTS

Our lives are made of contrasts
you and I, male and female
blue eyes and brown, yang and yin.

Forest green is greener against
blue sky made bluer.

In the wintertime of our love
fire cracks and glows,
frost has no chance to gather.

FROLIC

I tease that you can't keep up
you laugh when I stumble.

We walk the clouds
steady our balance touching the blue roof

clamber over, around, leap into pockets
discovery waits in the constant change.

We breathe lightly of thin air
give no thought to safety nets

lunch on billows of cream
champagne-flavored or vanilla.

We could love cradled in geodes –
white sapphire or blue

crystal without edges
spun soft as meringue.

We'd know the ecstasy of elevation
close to heaven.

Marie Gilbert

OF TIME AND THE ALPHABET BLOCKS

These past few days alone with you
have shown me time as substance
to be seen, to be touched.

Not time blocked off,
saved on a calendar,
but time as the block itself,

like the blocks children use
when they ABC at castle building.
In our time, G faced us.

An end grew heavy, a push from somewhere,
G toppled with scant sound.
Now I think it stood for grace,

the state from which I trace next the H
up and down the carved wood, across the horizontal
guessing – could be for hell or for heaven.

For each vertical down, fingers tell,
one of equal length points up
and each is an extension of the other.

OCTOBER, NOVEMBER, AND AFTER

Shafts of gold finger the land,
feel for the slowing of pulse.
I breathe the gold under blue, blue.
A heaviness slips over.

Now we walk under pale sun
leave long shadows.
Cold clutches bones
fills the marrow weary.

Gray days close down early
to kindling and logs
fireside
and flickering light.

Marie Gilbert

THREE STAGES OF ONE MAN

He swaggers in ready khaki
sees her quivering on limp knees
at the very edge of the jungle,
stops to clasp her hand,
it nestles his palm.

One hand for her
one wielding the machete
they lunge into the brush
slashing a path round about,
(there is no map) carving a space
for two, for three, for four.
Both hands hack the blade
her hands overflow, she pants beside him
through steaming verdancy. Trusting,
touching with eyes they strive
for the straight path in rampant jungle.

Near the far edge light filters
through thinning trees. In ease
he swings, a boy Tarzan, smiles
to see she sticks ever closer.
He slices paths on whim
on trial, follows in delight.

LONESOME BLOOD

A quiver of memory
and I feel your approach
hear footsteps that can only be
my blood pounding.

You leave me
a dusting of whispers.
Currents rise in stairwells
shadows quicken around doorways.

I lean into stirrings
stretch, strain against Earth bindings –
gravity and oxygen –
in search of ribs to circle

forearms to grasp –
happy to be grasped.
My hands hunger to walk
over responding flesh.

Marie Gilbert

NOW AND AGAIN

I awake to caresses,
as dew formed in the night
rouses the grass at dawn,
anoints hibiscus cups
holding still and wide.

Arising from such care
neither plants nor I could wilt
under pressure of heat
even white heat glancing,
but, revel in the day, the festival
and the light
until time to be gentled down
in its fading.

Marie Gilbert

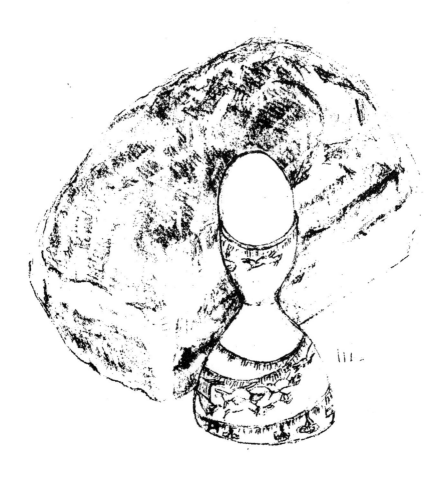

THE PARADOX OF BELONGING

You held the harness steady.
It rested lightly as I settled in
freely choosing to soft-boil the eggs
at 7:15 on the dot. You brought home
bread and bacon, mine to feed us.
I was free to share with a friend,
pack some off to Bangladesh, or
from some wild beach, feed it to the crying gulls.

When you were snatched away to war,
here where we had lived as four
I was free to choose for three of us
to wait for your return.

Twined in sinew
roped in the grasp of arms
freedom comes lighter than air
out, out to the sting of stars
pointing back to Earth.

Marie Gilbert

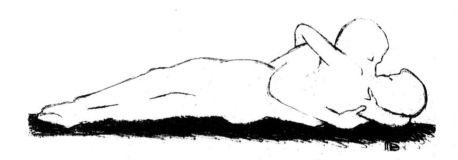

MORNING TIME IN BED

Cool jets of breath pulse my earlobes
and under my chin.
Your arm as a boa snuggles away the chill.

Blue skies dispel ground mist. I should rise.

I'll not be one to break the pleasure
of parts to parts. Your eyes will open soon
and you will say
what we should do.

Marie Gilbert

WHEN I HEAR THE SOUND

On nighthawk wings
you'll come
when I am devastated
lonely
beyond alone.

You will spill into night air
brake with wing feathers
on nearing Earth.

I will hear the sound
you taught me to hear,
clutch the pungent air,
soak up nearness
with every pore.

IN THE NIGHT DRIZZLE

The tall shadow is gone
from this playing ground
leaving keen–cut
silhouette sharper than life.

A sweater draping the swing strap
I am left
all through the night drizzle
dripping red from my weave.
With morning, the fabric will dry,
stiffen in the sun.

Marie Gilbert

AND WELCOME

My furnace door cracks
creates a draft
when you come.
Coals glow
flames rise
lick up to the top log.
Tongues blue, yellow, and red
seal the whimper in the throat.

Pale plums swirl
pure as gratitude.
Ruddy arms shift
log down onto log,
feather into the pit
fine ash
that fluffs away weightless,
leaves clean as hunger.

PART THREE

....gather yourselves from the shallows.

Marie Gilbert

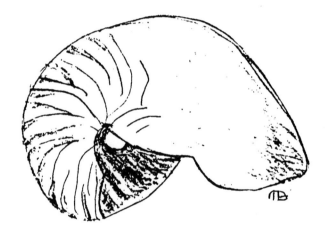

ROUNDNESS

I cannot reverse the process – learn to live in water –
even though I feel some ancient predecessor
slithered up on shore and learned to stay.

So this beach is the edge of the world.

I am tugged to wade knee–deep
thrill with the power of the rush
that empties the inlet into the sea

tugged to race towards waves
for the cold slap of spray,
tease off in rougher weather.

Prince Henry had the cliffs of Portugal
as a spine behind him.
My sanguine sand shifts obeisant to tide.

The moon pulls alike
the tide, Prince Henry, me
and Columbus, who trusted the curve,

could have found he sailed a tabletop
over something even heaven couldn't name
instead of roundness.

Even though we know the thrust
to puncture gravity and adjust an orbit,
vast circular paths remain inviolate.

As the child who rides his tricycle
round the block and back to home,
we trust roundness.

Marie Gilbert

OUT OF THE SEA

Mammal-mother rolled over quickly
after giving birth
flooded her pup alive
in the first sputtering breath of air.
Suckling
she fondled with flippers
even as she reveled
in watery arms.
Was there upheaval, or
did they stray too close,
find themselves
gravel scratching slick skins
bellying along
growing claws to dig footholds
in this place of dirt, sky and air.
Earth belched fire and steam
heaved them up on mountains.

They learned of corn and of meat,

suffered for salt,
sighed to the wind
singing sounds of sea.

Marie Gilbert

STORM WATCH ON WACCAMAW NECK

I hear a throaty rumble,
watch the sky grow bright
dark again
as black muscles bulge
to the north, east, west.

South breeze rules here
on the beach,
a cool river of air surprises me
spray scurries south to north along rollers
running on the slant.

Bright pulse thrills the air.
I breathe the light.
The storm strikes
west of the river
north along the coast
to strip a tree, rip a barn
splinter a mast out east at sea.

Such power raises the hair on my arms.
Blood flows thin and quick
I question my south breeze
no match for storm currents,
air masses.

Close overhead
veins of light etch the gray
like blood vessels on anatomy charts.
Energy up there does not charge to earth
– not yet.

Pure instinct pulls me
up from sand
hastens me home;

cheats me.

No lightning cracks
no rains come near

I could have stayed
and watched.

Marie Gilbert

PREFERENCE

Crusty with salt
stinging from sun after
dragging the shrimp net
raking clams
I skid the slope
down the dunes to the sea
to slip between waves and seaweed
part the cool water
refreshed
belonging.

High noon into night,
dune top to the sea
let it not be in December
when waves pounding the beach
cause sonic booms in the head
their frigid teeth gnaw
at toes and ankle bones
hoarfrosting the blood.

Damp with the sweat of August
may I squeeze between drops
head first
to be refreshed.

BUILDING SITE

Where boots know mud
the rhythm of shovels
first light to twilight,
nearly audible wondering rises,
"How long, which way out?"

Life began in a muddy bay
when Earth was shallow water.
One amoeba at a time prepared
to swim or to walk out of mud
whenever land sorted from sea.

"How long, how long?"
the shovels ring.
"Which way, which way?"
Boots suck the mud
squish, step along.

Marie Gilbert

DANCING IN NO MAN'S LAND

Spray flew up to touch the gulls,
gray waves gnawed the base of dunes.

The nor'easter blew out in the night.

The sea withdrew
leaving piles of dingy foam
spittle
to sink and stain the strand
to stake his claim.

I prance this widened beach,
with an eye on the listless waves,
kick my toe
at piles of foam.

THE EXPERIMENT

We swim out of the mouth of ocean
out of her deep belly.
Our curve of body straightens tall
to see an intriguing distance.
Blood surges with desire
to put to use all that lies before us:

tear open the breast of earth,
fence the field, train animals
to be ours or be hunted,
clear forests, quicken streams
build dams to stem the flow –
beavers can be used for fur.

Needs, solutions, needs
we are assigned to the knife edge
– life or death – to learn
where the slim lines fall.

So it is good to curl up
like a shrimp, float in saline
use the open sea's
full dome of vision.

Marie Gilbert

THE TELLING DREAM

Clear as June here on Myrtle Beach
a dream came to me last night asking
to be passed along while it is fresh
though I doubt it will ever grow stale.
Settle yourselves on the sand soft under the sun
and hear me. It begins when

I race out ankle deep
run back from the waves
foam licking my heels.
Again, and to the knee this time
a teasing retreat,
teasing though I have every intention
of swimming in this ocean,
gliding beneath the surface to feel
the flow on my smallness as it is given
to the great wholeness.

You, my friends, are near.
Our feet shuffle the sandy bottom
as we frolic in the water.
For no known reason, I am
a few feet further out.
Looking up I see a monster wave
not unlike the Great Wave Off Kanagawa
curve out of the sea
feather white fringe and dragon spray.

I grab a deep breath, go under
to the still water on the smooth sand floor,
hope you see the wave in time to duck,
are not pummeled in back bending turbulence.

I wait in the quiet water for the small surge
that signals all is clear above, surface,
bob about pleasantly in the chop
notice you were caught by the sudden wave
for you gather yourselves from the shallows.

My feet cannot reach the bottom.
I swim a few strokes shoreward
make no progress. I watch
for a wave on which to catch a ride.

The sea has changed: whitecaps flip
do not crest and roll to shore.
The current forms a sack
not to be broken by struggle.

And so I wait.
Someone will send a power boat
yet I know of none nearby.
Swim down the coast, I think,
find a counter current toward the beach.
There must be one.

Ahead is the Ocean Plaza Pier.
I have never been in water
so near this claw-like danger where
barnacled posts stand close ranked.
The pocket sweeps me along.
The fisherman on the pier grow clearer.
I wave an arm, give a yell for help
and once again, "Help!"

No need to waste strength.
As a child boxing with his father, this match
will be won only through charity.
Perhaps showing spunk is the key.
The salty lapping on my face seems benign.

Marie Gilbert

Extending beyond the usable pier
snaggle-toothed relics of hurricanes
hold up blood letting barnacles.
I will thread between those posts
make myself small
not fight the current, work with it
to slip through.

Midway the labyrinth
one post shines slick antiquity
unchosen even by barnacles.
I grasp its soggy support.

It breaks below the water line
happy for release to sink
would gladly take me with it.

I let it slip below,
continue to work with the mainstream.

Time holds its breath
until I see the last post behind me
discover the pocket disintegrated.

The game is over.

Waves head up, roll toward the beach.
I let them carry me,
nudge me on sliding foam
 leave me leaden on slick sand
at the rim of the sea.

"Foolish to swim so near the pier,"
states a passing walker.

WINDING DAY INTO NIGHT
ON THE CAROLINA COAST

Brightest is slick wet sand
returning peach and purple iridescence
to departing sun.

The fisherman closes his tackle box, his folding chair.
Dangling his string of blues, he follows
the bouncing tip of his surf rod
over the dunes.

The strand belongs to flashing red beaks
of Caspian terns and oystercatchers,
to masts of catamarans tall on the dunes,
halyards clanging lonesome in the wind.

In a copse of scrub oak
the fisherman cleans his blues,
scales lift to the last of the sun.

Lamplight leaks through shutter cracks
as he dredges his catch in cornmeal
fries it in bacon fat.

Hoot HOOT to woo waves in the day of owls
softly in their fluff hunting
marsh and field by sound and night sight.

Mice and rabbits scurry,
even the silence breathes claws and hooked beaks.

Marie Gilbert

I SALLY FORTH

The path back to mooring is foam
peeled port and starboard
wavering in the current
sponged away by the breeze.

So it's outward
set loose into the trackless.

Now
lightly on the mainsheet
deftly on the tiller
give an eye to the telltale

hang ready
to seize the moment.

Marie Gilbert

FORECAST

Hollow tunnels of sound bounce
off the stone cold sea wall.
West wind pleats horizon seam, blue to blue.

Waves flop on sand
slowly, smoothly
die echoing:

turn my pondering to hollow bones
to vibrations in the marrow
quivering with thought of return to water.

Being neither Greek nor Roman, Poseidon and Neptune
may flip cockles for remains, while
salvable parts float in vitreous drops

to gather as new life near some warm beach
where gel takes shape – small, mean, or fine
in the turn of time's economy with matter.

COMPARISON

As a ship
you're scuttled,
as a cup
you're overflowing.
Lifted from sand
you're the newest shell
in my collection.

Marie Gilbert

JUST ENOUGH

I walk the beach to the inlet south,
too wide to swim;
to the inlet north, treacherous current.

Within these small miles
waves and wind shift the sand,
a turtle crawls up, nests farther south.

Pelicans, willets, gulls, coquina
the busy rhythm flows. Outside the pull
today I struggle with thoughts

of one who fought for time
and lost to the claws of cancer.
I find a shell perfect in the human way
which is almost. It is his color.

I think of a young friend
who somehow cannot take up the gift of herself,
days slither through her fingers.

Far away in Sarajevo, new blood spills
on ancient animosities again unleashed
and again, leaves maimed children,
snipers shooting those who retrieve the dead.

On the stage of sand, gulls snatch and grab,
willets lunge for life of bone and feather,
earn just enough, again tomorrow, just enough.

our large brains wonder,
weep.

PART FOUR

....stride
through fog....

THE AFTER-RING

When the black depth of night is lavished
with buttons, some pierce near
large as brilliant saucers
some snap deep and snug

the hawk drags wing feathers
scoops food from air
jars through the night
folds into drugged sleep

as whip-poor-will, whip-poor-will's
urgent repetition pulls up a gauze of light
to chill the night to gray, to dim the stars.
Delighted birds of morning rise.

But I remember the velvet
remember the night's extravaganza
feel the hidden brilliance hover
to button heaven close to Earth.

Marie Gilbert

FINDING THE LINK

I shed my gloves;
fingers crumble earth, feel
the push and pull of energy,

the spade eases soil to part
carves a place in the coolness
and in the warmth
for the waiting hibiscus.

In the mix of roots to be cleared
one root stretches, bruises
refuses to sever
has no end
and no beginning –

I have struck a meridian
meshing Earth to ball shape
weaving over the Tropic of Capricorn
past a sheep station in the out back
through the steam of a gold mine in Africa

the meridian ducks under the Equator
near the River Nile or the Amazon

over the Tropic of Cancer
beside the Taj Mahal
through the black deep of Calcutta
wanders as a Bedouin in the empty quarter
rides with oil slick sheiks.

The grim thong grew tight
beneath the bombing of London
the bodies broken on Tian'anmen Square

under antarctic ice
under Latvian tundra – on
to knot a web
in the gray light at the poles.

Beneath indigo sky
my palm holds loam, and
this strained and bleeding link.

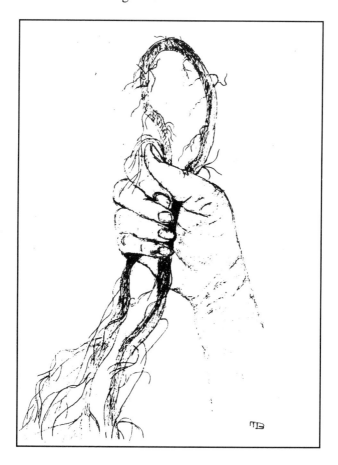

Marie Gilbert

INTO SPAIN AT BADAJOZ

Cork trees stripped blood red
olive cut to bone
bulls and bulls mile after mile

the desolation of Extremadura –
heat, cold, drought.
Born here could you ever
yearn for home.

We stop at the first human sign
in a hundred miles, a hostel
teeming, hot though it is.

A bride, radiant in rich satin
cool in the grace granted weddings
dances and dances with each guest

to the music of The Tuna
medieval in black velvet piped red.
We are welcome to sway, clap, and cheer;

to watch:
the pattern of the dance
glances freeze in memory

whispers seed the blood
come home, come home.

GRANDMOTHER'S DRESS

Long it had lain in the tissue
yet flows alive from the box,
velvet eager to pour emerald
over its young lady
augmenting her every move.

Leg-o-mutton sleeves taper
to points on backs of hands
wishing to be kissed,
the neck snuggles
the skirt swishes, wanting to waltz
and the waist shapes in, in, in.

"Try it," Mother says
eyeing me at fifteen,
"It would be lovely
for the costume party."

Holding my breath I ease in
to leave a bare vee where jet buttons
should close the back.

"People were smaller then,"
Mother consoles,
"and girls wore corselets."

To shrink I would gladly sip
from Wonderland's bottle
or fan with Alice's fan!

We speak of letting out seams ...
but, no, leave it gentled in the box
to follow slowly after
the girl who wore it dancing.

Marie Gilbert

RACCOON MOTHER

Northeast wind curses the night
after the noonday we ripped chimney boxing
to expose the nest
the raccoon gnawed
through cedar siding to build.

The lady from Animal Control
lifted each baby up to her chin
called for a heating pad, a warm box.
"Two girls and a boy!" she announced
proud as if she had delivered them.

The mother peeped from high in the gaping hole,
"I'll come for her tomorrow,
raise these babes myself if she doesn't
take this yummy-smelly cat food trail."
She spooned dollops leading into the trap.

This stormy night does mother weep,
avoid traps in bloody desperation,
return by instinct to the same spot
each April, demolish our house
planned rustic as woods to blend our worlds

and did this lead her on?
Our worlds grind and crush.

Let me talk about the delicate line
while we watch
as she lives out
whatever she must.

Marie Gilbert

SHARING WITH DEER

Somewhere in the whistle of the wind
this wild night that is still August
deer nose from bush to bush antlers heavy
fawns scamper in the pattern set –

twins born under the live oak last May.
From high on the porch we watched
the mother lick, clean
urge them up on wobbly legs

bed them down side by side, head to tail
just off the walk under the low pines.
She left to do what she must,
feed after giving birth.

Long vacant times at this house
mean the deer own it as much as we,
even eat the buds on juniper
planted as one thing deer ignore.

Close to the walks, to the windows
fawns with spots nearly faded, nibble;
ears stiffen, heads freeze at alert
for human sounds of slammings, callings.

Here, we need to live quietly.

FLAMENCO ON THE GUADALQUIVIR RIVER

The guitar builds a fullness
with a life of its own
reverberates from twelve strings
to charge each crack of air we breathe.

The voice comes up from viscera
seethes through the chest, absorbs pulse
catches in throat restrictions
released in swells of rhythm.

Castanets high, the dancer, lean as eel
sways and slithers
subdued with stomp click
stomp click click to hammer a throb.

The wellspring of Spain pours
sparks fling from eye to eye
within the triangle of Gypsies
feeding each other to bursting.

Quick creation surpasses the sum
as breathless we witness
"Duende"
the bright mist whispers, "Duende!"

Marie Gilbert

NIGHT CONNECTION

The full moon gives life to the Oriental rug
abracadabra on October night.
On the floor of the bedroom
luminescence bright enough to singe
entices the fingers to chance
the glow so like active dust,
push the nap to darken, lighten
feel it push back.

Under the same moon
sheep once lay at meadow,
wool washed and carded
dried under a sky of stars.

The pattern took shape in someone's mind
flowed through the fingers
the knotting at the loom.

A camel perhaps watched
or a sheep who knew the wool.

With the tent flap up
flies bothered the baby,
or, buttoned against the wind
the baby cuddled in sheepskin.

I revel in this near to living creation
sense a connection
bounced off the moon.

ON TAKING CARE OF TALENT

With care she gathers her talent
funnels it into the perfect jar
to place up high on the shelf.

She fumbles and spills some
over the edge of the jar.
The earth where it falls grows flowers.

Marie Gilbert

TEMPLE OF POSEIDON

Even on the map
the finger that is Cape Sounion
beckons.

The road
flirts with the water's edge,
lifts to the promontory.

Byron carved his name
in the stone of this temple
early in eighteen hundred.

A sailor from Finland
dated his name early seventeen –
not long ago as time is reckoned here.

Given the slice of time to sail round Europe
I wonder if he planned his journey as I did
or chanced to see this temple,

anchored his sail below
climbed this cliff to pay respects
or to get his bearings.

I believe Byron and the Finn
quivered as I do now,
sky Aegean blue behind Doric columns,

columns that stretch no less grand
as measures of the ground;
offering to the sun,

silence, the silence of stone
patient with rain and
circles of time.

From the rude dawning, Agamemnon, Mycenae,
the wars, to Pericles
the tongue pushed against darkness.

KICKING THE TRACES

At the feet of August
an untimely burst brings
rain to green
wind to fleece and spin the clouds
cool to spell the pounding wrist of summer.
Rules are broken in caprice
as a dutiful mother
without warning
wakes her sleeping babe, and
clasping the cackling child
runs loose through open fields
to meet head-on
a wind too fresh.

Marie Gilbert

TRANSITION

At Hampton Plantation, blue twill
of a Park Service uniform bunches
about his wiry frame.
Dark polished leather stretches
to cover his fleshless face.

From white, white orbs, his small eyes
once keen for game and camouflaged snakes,
alert to trigger quick response when hunting
with Colonel Rutledge, still snap
but the snap is small
and it is slow.

He glimpses where he is going,
speaks with the Colonel and Missy,
sees them hover about the porch roof
when the house breathes in the evening.

While he waits
he smiles
nods to visitors,
opens the heavy door.

EASTER SUNDAY

Beside a pond where beer cans float
tossed from passing car windows,
where traffic soon will rumble the bridge

alone I seek signs
of the promise.

The joy of cathedral bells bathes the water
and I know pipe organs swell
Hallelujah rings from pulpits.

On green tended hillsides,
choirs sing "He is risen"
in this same first light that cleanses me.

I seek signs here,
trust against disappointment.

Springtime maples swell blood drops.
Willow's nascent trailings brush murky water.
A mostly mallard swims out from under.

Strangely representative she seems
as she coaxes her mottled brood of three
to take to the water.

Marie Gilbert

SUMMONS TO THE WELL

The clock strikes out of smothering night
stretched long between hours.

Stop and listen.
A full Celtic voice intones,
hangs my name on the air
to be heard again, again.

I slip from bed to window.
Moonlight on brown grass imitates snow,
rainbows halo lampposts.
The street slumbers dark and empty.
Silence brews a thick gruel.

Echoes ride with horseman
who gallop the night sky.

Flat in bed I tug the mind tape
up out of the well
study the film
in search of bubbles, yeasty bubbles.

THE GREATER THREAT

For those who bask in noonday sun
for those who hug the fireside
there has to be a counterpart to hell –
hoarfrosted demons with visible breath
poking frozen pitchforks at ice floes
that grind and crack in crunching lakes
of quivering, simpering, souls.

Marie Gilbert

SPIDER FALL

Sheer spun is the thread holding
our individual spider dangling
swaying precariously – our deadly spider

venom tailored to chill our special blood,
legs a length to fit our shoulders
tighten the throat, still the pounding heart.

Along beneath the trees
open arms embracing what comes
no need to strain deciphering manes

on spiders swinging in gossamer suspension
from branches growing winter bare.
When leaves slip, catch each bright finality

with your eyes if not with your hands,
the spider that drops, will fall
when spiders will.

ON WATCHING CHALLENGER
January 28, 1986

The crew of seven seeks
the ultimate stretch
out beyond the strings of Earth

to find whatever waits
for man's bringing home
to pyramid science.

Half the State of Florida stands
face up on a clear, cold morning
to watch in animal numbness

as awesome surge of red
bleeds orange
colorless

a cloud of vapor
grows long fingers that grasp
for Earth in the habit of gravity.

Inch of bone, shred of sock wash ashore
dredges haul debris from ocean depth –
outgrown shell discarded.

The cloud of vapor floats free
in pure space beyond tomorrow.

Marie Gilbert

THE DAY THE SUN DID NOT COME UP

Birds weary of silence
clutch twigs
wait for the pre-light signal
theirs alone to hear.

Crickets having rehearsed
all through the night
tune up again
to fill the empty air.

I write creeping fear.

Loosed from Sun we hurtle the dark
lost, cold, colder, closing down
black, deeper black
for days, a month? No more.

Here the cosmic poem ends.

The newsboy follows his flashing beam
explains why he is early –
the storm last night
jumped his clock ahead by hours.

And, yes, indeed, the same is true of mine!

Dash out to the East
to meet returning light,
innocent as a naked savage
praise the sun.

TO SHAKE THE WINTER NADIR

When day comes colorless, black to light,
grays swirl, hover
over silver wrinkles in the bay –

silver-hold that bright thought,
ride the South bridge
drive on in the rain
until the sun soaks through.

Somewhere,
rains come only past midnight
low moons hang sultry
rhythms weave soft air, and
hugs come of a sudden.

Look South to blunt jagged edges
set bare feet firmly on sterling rails.

Marie Gilbert

DEALING WITH TREASURE

I pause to look up the attic stair
at stacks of corrugated boxes –
the dusty fingers point to rafters,
through the roof and beyond.

Pride in ancestors flogs me
to unleash the bastions –
square-knotted, hemp twined
labeled in grease pencil
clear only to one long gone –
to embellish the present
from the store house of the past:

Crumbling letters written at Verdun
or on the Oregon Trail – to read
and to preserve. French lace cloth
Madeira napkins yellow for soap and sun,
unfinished patchwork quilt,
baby dresses too fine to discard
too fragile to use,
crystal goblets in threes, a wedding gown,
ancestral photographs like puzzles to solve,
souvenir spoons, tarnished and bent, wondrous
with inscriptions and dates to decipher,
shoe buttoners, shaving mugs, bobbins
a jeweled broach without a clasp
lace fans, and earrings one of a kind.

Once out, those treasures demand attention
or, their cocoons opened, gauze wings sizzle
as in candle light, and disintegrate.
Hands filled with fragile value
relish the feel, though cluttered helpless
to the tick of hours, days.

Future strides into present.
I push the attic door shut.
Let dust fall upon dust.

Marie Gilbert

SUBTLE RHYTHMS
(observation on returning to North Carolina)

In South Florida
spring slips in barely noticed
having been gone so short a span.
Soft air touches
smells of humus, verdancy and blossom.

Carolina spring
holds its breath.
Under sheds, tractors stand
ready to lurch into fields still puddled.
Mast squishes on the forest floor.
Oak and pine clutch yellow dust
in hair-triggered fingers.
Children's toes twitch
ready to hop out of shoes.
Brown grasses tease
admit to no green intentions.

Steeped in the rhythm of this ritual
I catch a quickening pulse
turn out to inspect minutiae
so subtle the fattening bud.

THE COMPLETE WOMAN IS NOT TOPIARY

Just last summer
pickles and plum jelly
permeated the house with
pungent spice and sweet vinegar.

In the spring
Cub Scouts trooped in
with clattering tuna cans and paint
to make hurricane lamps.

Back last winter
quilt scraps billowed, calico leaves
covering tabletops,
drifting with dust beneath.

I'd wonder, but
this autumn day I see
the sweet gum –
a patch of purple
a branch of gold
a clump of crimson –
plough new sky
tall above the forest.

Marie Gilbert

FINAL BEE

A bee settled on my blanket
looking for flowers.
A red line flowed about his back
just outside the scroll
etched white on shining black.

Quite marvelous, this bee.
I felt certain he had no sting.
He flew away leaving me sure
he would fly back again one day,

settle on my blanket of flowers
sip from lovely blossoms.
A red line would flow just inside
the empty hour glass
etched clean white on shining black.

He came again this April
buzzing stressed syllables
to my attention, plastering
long kisses on the glass door.

I would never wave this bee away
nor would I dare to crack the door.

Not this April.

Marie Gilbert

INSIGHT IN FOG

On yesterday's sunlit beach
I would have marveled at my stride
through fog toward nothing I can see;
much as clarity in another world
might note our daily walk in lesser light
toward what we can only guess.

Gulls and pelicans gray and grayer
flocks mixed in undistinguishing air,
dune grass bland as noodles
even my green jacket seems softened to a blur
since birds do not fly up at my passing.
They rise in low, short flights
as if loath to lose sight of their beach.

On a trackless moor I'd be lost.
Along the shore I am down the beach
from home now vanished
sightless as the air ahead.
A blur of color in a flow of gray,
fog folds me into itself
in this moment of clarity.

ABOUT THE AUTHOR

Marie Gilbert was born in Florence, South Carolina where she lived during her public school years. At Rollins College, she pursued a dual major in English and Psychology, and upon graduation also received the Algernon Sydney Sullivan Medallion. This is her fifth published collection. Her work appears in Reviews and Anthologies in the United States, Ireland, and Japan. In 1987 and again in 1990, she won the Lyric Poem Prize awarded by the Poetry Society of South Carolina.

She has served the North Carolina Poetry Society in many capacities, from 1990 to 1992, as President. She is listed with the North Carolina Writers Conference, and is a member of Friday Noon Poets and Writer's Group of the Triad. Recently, she gave a reading of her poetry at the Dock Street Theatre Court Yard under the auspices of the Charleston, S.C. Office of Cultural Affairs.

She and her husband have lived in South Carolina, Illinois, Missouri, Ohio and now divide time between Greensboro, N.C. and Georgetown, S.C.. They have a son, a daughter, and four granddaughters.